Coffee Creations

Rio Nuevo Publishers®

P.O. Box 5250, Tucson, Arizona 85703-0250

(520) 623-9558, www.rionuevo.com

Text and photography © 2008 by Rio Nuevo Publishers.
Food styling by Tracy Vega.

Photography credits as follows:
dreamstime.com: front cover, page 26.
W. Ross Humphreys: page 38.
Marilyn Noble: pages 3, 9, 12, 15, 45, and 75 (all taken
at Doka Estate, Alajuela, Costa Rica).
Robin Stancliff: back cover, pages 4, 5, 16, 19, 23, 29,
34, 37, 41, 48, 51, 55, 59, 62, 68, 71, and 72.

Library of Congress Cataloging-in-Publication Data

Grimes, Gwin Grogan.
Coffee creations / Gwin Grogan Grimes.
      p. cm. -- (Cook west series)
Includes index.
ISBN 978-1-933855-11-0
1. Cookery (Coffee) I. Title.
TX819.C6G75 2007
641.6'373--dc22

                                        2007024398

Design: Karen Schober, Seattle, Washington.
Printed in Korea.

10 9 8 7 6 5 4 3 2 1

coffee

creations

GWIN GROGAN GRIMES

RIO NUEVO PUBLISHERS
TUCSON, ARIZONA

contents

introduction

Coffee has a long, rich history, beginning with its discovery in its native habitat of Ethiopia, also known then as the Kingdom of Kaffa. A number of books have been written about coffee, from its cultivation to trading to coffeehouses, but what I'm interested in is *cooking* with coffee.

Coffee is incredibly versatile, as delicious in a mug as it is when made into a sweet dessert or savory marinade for meat. I've included recipes for some popular coffee drinks, both hot and cold, to make at home, as well as breakfast dishes, entrées, sides, and, of course, plenty of desserts. Coffee shines in desserts because it pairs so well with the classic flavors of chocolate and vanilla, but its earthy, smoky flavors accent savory dishes, too.

But first things first: In order to cook with coffee, you've got to make good coffee. One thing I've learned in my research and testing for this cookbook is that most people have very specific requirements for their morning cup. (It's one explanation for those long lines at the coffeehouse!)

You can't make a superior product with inferior ingredients, so let's start with the beans. Buy your beans as freshly roasted as possible. That means buying from a local roaster or from a store with a lot of turnover. Buy small amounts and store them away from light and heat (the two enemies of coffee). Coffee beans can go bad when the natural oils in them turn rancid.

Experts say that the freezer is acceptable for long-term storage of beans, but never, ever keep them in the refrigerator, where they may pick up offensive odors (again, because the oils in the beans carry aromas and flavors) or become excessively moist. If you don't have a local supplier, try two of my favorites: Jessica's Biscuit (www.jessicasbiscuit.com or 800-878-4264) and Zingerman's (www.zingermans.com or 888-636-8162).

Buy small amounts of coffee beans until you find the brews you like best. Be aware that many of the beans in flavored coffees are coated in artificial flavors, so read labels carefully. Coffee beans are available in prices ranging from bargain to ultra-expensive, but cost doesn't always equal quality. Many supermarket brands are blends made to ensure consistency from batch to batch. Some connoisseurs prefer only Hawaiian or Colombian or African beans. Like fine wine, coffee marketers are offering single-estate beans (coffee grown on a single plantation instead of a blend from all over a country, region, or the world). "Fair trade" coffees help ensure that coffee growers and workers are paid a living wage. The coffee world is interesting, diverse, and incredibly flavorful.

The only other ingredient in coffee is water, so consider what comes out of your tap. Do you like the way it tastes? Does it taste fresh, clean, and free of chemicals and other unpleasant tastes and aromas? If not, use bottled, still water to make your coffee.

Grind your beans as close to brewing time as reasonable. As soon as the beans are ground, they begin losing freshness and flavor. Small blade grinders are inexpensive (less than $20), but they can grind the beans unevenly, and they generate heat, which can cause the coffee to taste burned. Also, most are not big enough to grind enough beans at a time for a pot of coffee.

Most coffee aficionados, like my friend Heather (a true connoisseur and an inspiration for this book), recommend burr grinders, which don't generate as much heat and create a more consistent grind than the smaller blade grinders. They are more expensive (beginning at about $50) and take up more counter space, however. The advantage of an even grind is that

more of the surface area of the coffee beans is exposed to the water during brewing, creating a better cup of coffee. If you are in the market for a new coffee grinder, you may want to research the advantages and disadvantages of conical burr grinders versus wheel burr grinders.

Good coffee can be made in automatic drip makers, percolators, French presses, and espresso machines, both stovetop and automatic. Coffee lovers usually develop a preference for a particular method. Automatic drip makers are the most popular machines and are available in a wide range of sizes, prices, and quality, from single-cup makers to 12-cup behemoths with thermal pots. Old-fashioned percolators make strong brews and have their adherents among traditionalists. The French press has its own fan club, but it doesn't keep the coffee hot after it has been brewed.

Espresso machines are designed to make the strong coffee popularized by the Italians. (Espresso, by the way, is not a type of coffee, it's a grind—a very fine grind. Any coffee can be ground to espresso.) Simple stovetop pots are available in many sizes to make one cup at a time to many, and can cost anywhere from about $12 to $50. The automatic electric machines start at about $50 and go up—way up, into the thousands—but are the ultimate in high-performance coffee.

Once you've got the beans and equipment covered, then the only thing left to discuss is technique. Most experts recommend six ounces of water for every two tablespoons of coffee. That may be a little strong for some folks, so adjust accordingly. For the recipes in this book, however, the coffee was brewed in the standard six ounces to two tablespoon ratio.

Instant coffee is a relatively new invention, just over a hundred years old. While most coffee fans would not willingly trade their cups of freshly brewed java for a cup of instant, instant coffee makes a great ingredient for cooking and baking. Instant coffee is, generally speaking, dehydrated brewed coffee. In some recipes I advise pressing the coffee through a fine-mesh strainer as the crystals are sometimes rather large.

Another great convenience product that works well in baking is a type of instant coffee called espresso powder. I use an Italian brand called Medaglia d'Oro that I can buy at the supermarket. If it's not available in yours, it can be purchased from baking suppliers such as the King Arthur Flour Baker's Catalogue (www.kingarthurflour.com or 800-777-4434.)

TIPS & TECHNIQUES

The best dishes begin with the freshest, highest quality ingredients. Always check expiration dates when available.

Measure accurately. Use a graduated set of cups for dry ingredients. Spoon the item into the cup and level off with a table knife or the handle of a wooden spoon. Use a liquid cup measure for liquid ingredients, checking the liquid at eye level. Use graduated measuring spoons for smaller measures, not flatware for the table.

For the greatest success in replicating these recipes, follow the instructions. Sounds simple, but it isn't always easy—especially if we're in a hurry. Read through the recipe, then gather the ingredients, and read through it again, all the way through. Make sure you are allowing enough time for all the steps. I always advise making the recipes as written the first time, then feel free to adapt and improvise!

Try this cooking-school secret: Get out all the ingredients you'll need for a recipe, then measure everything out and place it on a cookie sheet or tray. This is called *mise en place,* and it's

what professional chefs do to keep their workspace organized. You're less likely to forget an ingredient, and cooking will go so much more smoothly and faster if all the ingredients are measured out and ready to go when you are.

You won't need any fancy equipment or tools to prepare any of the recipes in this book, just a few knives, some pots, cookie sheets, and other baking pans. I use an outdoor gas grill extensively, all year long, in my mild Texas climate, but you could use charcoal or, for indoor cooking, a grill pan.

I recommend most home cooks start out with three basic knives: a chef's knife that's comfortable for you to use, which could be a blade length anywhere from six inches to twelve inches; a paring knife, three or four inches; and a serrated bread knife. You can accomplish many kitchen tasks with just these three knives.

INGREDIENTS

For my recipes, unless otherwise specified, the ingredients are:

Baking soda and *baking powder* are not interchangeable, although baking powder does contain some baking soda. Always check expiration dates, as both are leaveners.

Butter is unsalted butter. Store butter well-wrapped in the refrigerator so that it is less likely to pick up odors and flavors. For longer storage, wrap in foil and then place in a freezer bag, and store in the freezer.

Chocolate is good-quality baking chocolate or baking chips. For melting, use baking bars, not chips. Chocolate chips are manufactured with less cocoa butter in order to remain in chip shape during baking. Avoid using "chocolate bark" or other imitation chocolate in baking, because the cocoa butter in these products has been replaced with vegetable oils.

Cocoa is unsweetened cocoa powder, not sweetened hot chocolate mix. Available as "natural" or "Dutch process." Dutch-process cocoa is treated with an alkaline, has a milder taste, and is good to eat raw. Natural cocoa is untreated and slightly bitter. It is an excellent baking ingredient and gives brownies and cakes a deep chocolate flavor.

Dried herbs and ground spices should be purchased in small quantities. Write the date on the bottle or package and discard after one year. Store away from heat and light to retain flavor.

Flour is unbleached, all-purpose flour.

Nuts are toasted before adding to a recipe. Place in a dry skillet and cook over medium heat until nuts are very lightly browned and the aroma is apparent.

Pepper is freshly ground black pepper.

Salt is kosher salt. Its large crystal structure means that it has more volume than regular table salt, and you won't confuse it with sugar.

Sugar is pure cane sugar. If the package is not marked, it is likely beet sugar, and it may react differently in some candy recipes.

Vanilla is pure vanilla extract, not imitation. The fruit of a rain-forest orchid, real vanilla is expensive but worth it. Imitation extracts are a byproduct from wood pulp processing. Read labels before purchasing.

Yeast is active dry yeast sold in small packets or jars in the baking aisle of the supermarket.

Mocha

xxxxxx

A coffeehouse specialty you can make at home.

Serves 1

Fill a mug with hot tap water and let it sit for about a minute. Pour out the water and immediately add the coffee. Stir in half-and-half, chocolate syrup, and sugar to taste, if desired.

6 ounces hot, brewed coffee

2 tablespoons half-and-half, heated

2 tablespoons chocolate syrup

Sugar (optional)

Coffee-Spiked Coffee

xxxxxx

When you can't decide between an after-dinner drink or coffee, have both.

Serves 1

Fill a mug with hot tap water and let it sit for about a minute. Pour out the water and immediately add the coffee. Stir in coffee liqueur and, if desired, sugar and cream to taste.

6 ounces hot, brewed coffee

1½ ounces coffee liqueur

Sugar and cream (optional)

Va-Va-Vanilla Espresso (pictured)

xxxxxx

Serves 1

Vanilla is the world's most popular flavor, and here it helps mellow the strong espresso.

4 ounces hot, brewed espresso

½ cup half-and-half, warmed

½ teaspoon vanilla extract

2 teaspoons sugar (optional)

Fill a mug with hot tap water and let it sit for about a minute. Pour out the water and immediately add the espresso. Stir in half-and-half, vanilla, and, if desired, sugar to taste.

Thai-Mex Coffee

xxxxxx

Serves 1

My husband loves to order Café Sua Da *in Vietnamese restaurants. This version adds a cinnamon accent to the classic.*

6 ounces hot, strong brewed coffee (preferably chicory coffee)

2 teaspoons sweetened condensed milk

1 Mexican cinnamon stick

Fill a mug with hot tap water and let it sit for about a minute. Pour out the water and immediately add the coffee. Stir in sweetened condensed milk with the cinnamon stick. Serve with the cinnamon stick in the coffee as a garnish.

Cinnamon Espresso

xxxxxx

Serves 1

4 ounces hot,
brewed espresso

2 tablespoons
half-and-half

1 drop cinnamon oil

Sugar (optional)

Cinnamon oil can be found with candy-making supplies at supermarkets and craft stores. It is very strong, so be sure to add only one drop at a time.

Fill a mug with hot tap water and let it sit for about a minute. Pour out the water and immediately add the espresso. Stir in half-and-half, cinnamon oil, and, if desired, sugar to taste.

Chocolate-Covered Caramel

xxxxxx

Serves 1

4 ounces hot,
brewed espresso

4 ounces half-and-
half, warmed

1 tablespoon caramel syrup
or ice-cream topping

1 tablespoon
chocolate syrup

Chocolate and caramel pair extremely well with espresso in this coffeehouse-inspired drink.

Fill a mug with hot tap water and let it sit for about a minute. Pour out the water and immediately add the espresso. Stir in half-and-half, caramel syrup or ice-cream topping, and chocolate syrup.

Mocha Milkshake

xxxxxx

Fast-food shakes will never taste the same after you try this rich smoothie at home.

Place the coffee, milk, ice cream, cinnamon, and ¼ cup of ice cubes in the jar of an electric blender. Cover and puree until smooth, adding more ice cubes, if necessary, to achieve a creamy consistency.

Serves 1

½ cup brewed coffee, cooled

¼ cup whole milk

½ cup premium chocolate ice cream

1 teaspoon cinnamon

About ¼–½ cup ice cubes (I use 2–5 cubes)

Café au Lait Smoothies

xxxxxx

Cool down on a hot day with this coffee-flavored frappé.

Place the milk, condensed milk, caramel syrup, coffee crystals, vanilla, and ½ cup of ice cubes in the jar of an electric blender. Cover and puree until smooth, adding more ice cubes, if necessary, to achieve a creamy consistency.

Serves 4

2 cups whole milk

14 ounces sweetened condensed milk

1 cup caramel syrup or ice cream topping

¼ cup instant coffee crystals

1 tablespoon vanilla extract

½–1 cup ice cubes

Adobe-Slide

xxxxxx

Serves 2

A Southwestern take on the popular mudslide drink.

1 ½ ounces vanilla-
flavored vodka

1 ½ ounces Mexican
coffee liqueur

1 ½ ounces Irish
cream liqueur

1 tablespoon chocolate
syrup, plus additional for
garnish (optional)

1–1 ½ cups ice cubes

Whipped cream, for
garnish (optional)

Place the vodka, Mexican coffee liqueur, Irish cream liqueur, chocolate syrup, and 1 cup of ice cubes in the jar of an electric blender. Cover and puree until smooth, adding more ice cubes, if necessary, to achieve a creamy consistency. Drizzle the insides of the serving glasses with chocolate syrup. Pour the mixture into the glasses and garnish with whipped cream, if desired.

Coffee Martini (pictured)

xxxxxx

Serves 1

Try various coffee liqueurs, as well as flavored vodkas, to vary this drink.

Ice

1 ½ ounces coffee liqueur

1 ½ ounces vodka

1 coffee bean

Fill a martini shaker with ice. Pour in the coffee liqueur and vodka and shake. Strain into a chilled martini glass and garnish with a coffee bean.

Irish Coffee

xxxxxx

Serves 1

1 cup hot,
brewed coffee

1½ ounces Irish
cream liqueur

1½ ounces Irish whiskey

Whipped cream

Pinch of freshly
ground nutmeg

Nothing beats the flavor of freshly grated nutmeg, and whole spices stay fresher for much longer than the pre-ground variety.

Pour the coffee into a serving mug. Stir in Irish cream liqueur and Irish whiskey. Top with whipped cream and sprinkle on a pinch of nutmeg.

Mexican Coffee

xxxxxx

Serves 1

1½ ounces Mexican
coffee liqueur

1 cup hot,
brewed coffee

Sugar

Whipped cream for
garnish (optional)

Buy the smallest bottles of several brands of coffee liqueur to find the one you like best; I prefer Kahlúa, which is made with Mexican coffee beans. You can also make your own, using the recipe on page 69.

Pour the coffee liqueur into a serving mug. Fill with hot, brewed coffee and sugar to taste. Garnish with whipped cream, if desired.

Grown-Up Mocha-Chocolate "Milk"

XXXXXX

This is not for the faint of heart.

Serves 2

Fill a cocktail shaker with ice and add coffee, chocolate, hazelnut, and Irish cream liqueurs. Shake and strain into cocktail glasses. Sift a little cocoa powder on top.

Ice

1½ ounces coffee liqueur

1½ ounces chocolate liqueur

1½ ounces hazelnut liqueur

1½ ounces Irish
cream liqueur

Cocoa powder, for garnish

Coffee for Breakfast
XXXXXX

Mocha-Nana Chip Muffins

xxxxxx

This is my family's favorite. Make sure to leave the bananas slightly lumpy for the best texture and flavor, and use an ice cream scoop to portion out the batter into muffin pans.

Preheat the oven to 350 degrees F. Line your muffin pan with paper or foil cups. Spray the cups with non-stick cooking spray. (This prevents the muffins from sticking to the paper.)

Beat the butter and sugar with an electric mixer until fluffy and light-colored. Add the egg, bananas, coffee, and vanilla, mixing just until incorporated. Mixture will look lumpy and curdled.

In another bowl, whisk together the flour, salt, baking soda, and baking powder. Add to the liquid mixture, then gently stir in the chocolate chips. Divide batter equally among the muffin tins, no more than two-thirds full, and bake in the preheated oven for 18–20 minutes or until a wooden skewer inserted in the center of a muffin comes out clean.

Variation: To make into loaves, coat three 8 x 4-inch pans with nonstick cooking spray. Bake in a preheated oven for about 35–50 minutes or until a wooden skewer inserted in the center of the loaves comes out clean.

Makes 18 muffins

Cooking spray

¼ **cup unsalted butter, softened**

1¼ **cups sugar**

1 **egg, slightly beaten**

3 **ripe bananas, peeled and broken into large chunks**

1 **teaspoon instant coffee, dissolved in 1 tablespoon hot water**

1 **teaspoon vanilla extract**

2¼ **cups all-purpose flour**

¼ **teaspoon salt**

1 **teaspoon baking soda**

1 **teaspoon baking powder**

1 **cup semisweet chocolate chips**

Cappuccino Swirl Bread

xxxxxx

½ cup unsalted butter, plus extra for pan

2 cups all-purpose flour, plus extra for pan

¼ teaspoon baking soda

¼ teaspoon baking powder

½ teaspoon salt

1¼ cups sugar

1 teaspoon vanilla extract

3 eggs

1 cup plain yogurt

¼ cup instant flavored cappuccino mix (such as English toffee)

My favorite recipe! I wanted to see how some of the new convenience coffee products would work in baked goods, and I was delighted.

Preheat the oven to 350 degrees F. Coat bottom only of a 9 x 5-inch loaf pan with butter and sprinkle with flour. Shake out excess flour.

In a bowl, whisk together the 2 cups of flour with the baking soda, baking powder, and salt. In another bowl, with an electric mixer, beat the ½ cup of butter and the sugar together until fluffy and light colored. Mix in the vanilla. Add the eggs, one at a time, mixing well after each. Add about one third of the flour mixture and beat until smooth. Add about one third of the yogurt and again beat until smooth. Repeat with the remaining flour and yogurt. Scoop out about 1 cup of the batter, stir the instant cappuccino mix into it, and set aside.

Pour half of the unflavored batter into the prepared pan. Drop the coffee-flavored batter by tablespoons onto the unflavored batter in the pan. Pour the remaining unflavored batter on top. With the handle of a wooden spoon, gently swirl the two batters together. Place in a preheated oven and bake for about 1 hour and 15 minutes or until a toothpick inserted into the center of the loaf comes out clean. Allow to cool for about 10 minutes, then slide a table knife around the edges of the loaf to loosen it. Remove the loaf from the pan and allow it to cool completely on a wire rack.

Coffee-Glazed Bacon

xxxxxx

Makes 16–20 slices

1 pound thick-sliced bacon

1 cup packed brown sugar

¼ cup brewed coffee

Cooking bacon in the oven is an old restaurant and caterers' trick. It makes much less mess than frying, and the bacon comes out crisp and perfectly cooked.

Preheat the oven to 350 degrees F. Place a wire cooling rack inside a baking pan with sides, such as a 15 x 10-inch jelly-roll pan.

Arrange the bacon slices on the rack. Place in the oven and bake for 10 minutes. Meanwhile, mix the brown sugar and coffee in a small bowl. Remove the bacon from the oven and brush about half the brown sugar–coffee mixture over it. Return the bacon to the oven and bake for 10 more minutes. Remove and turn over the bacon slices with a pair of tongs. Brush with the remaining brown sugar–coffee mixture. Bake for another 15 minutes or until the bacon is crisp and completely cooked.

Coffee Cinnamon Rolls

xxxxxx

Rich yeast rolls topped with a coffee and cream-cheese icing.

Makes 12

1 package (¼ ounce) active dry yeast

1 cup milk, warmed to 105–115 degrees F

4 cups all-purpose flour, plus more for dusting work surface

½ cup sugar

1 teaspoon salt

⅓ cup unsalted butter, melted and cooled

2 eggs, lightly beaten

1 cup packed brown sugar

2½ teaspoons ground cinnamon

½ cup unsalted butter, softened

Cooking spray

4 ounces cream cheese, softened

¼ cup unsalted butter, softened

1½ cups powdered sugar

1 teaspoon instant coffee, dissolved in 1 tablespoon hot water

1 teaspoon vanilla extract

Stir the dry yeast into the warm milk and set aside until the mixture is bubbly. In a large bowl, mix the flour, sugar, salt, ⅓ cup of butter, and eggs. Add the yeast-milk mixture and combine until a rough dough is formed.

Dust a work surface with flour. Remove the dough from the bowl and knead by folding the dough in half, then pressing away from your body with the heels of your hands. Fold the dough again, make a quarter turn, then press again. Repeat until the dough is smooth and soft. Form into a ball.

Place a little bit of flour in a large bowl and place the ball of dough inside. Cover with plastic wrap and let rise in a draft-free place for about an hour, or until the dough has doubled.

Dust your work surface with flour. Remove the dough from the bowl, gently pressing on it to remove air. Let it rest on the work surface, covered, for about 5 minutes. Roll out the dough into a rectangle about a quarter-inch thick. It will be about 20 inches long and about 16 inches wide. If the dough wants to shrink back as you roll it, stop and let it rest for about 5 minutes before continuing to roll.

To make the filling, combine the brown sugar, cinnamon, and ½ cup of butter in a bowl. Spread the mixture evenly over the dough rectangle.

Coat a baking pan with nonstick cooking spray. Roll up the dough, jelly-roll style, starting with a long side. Pinch together the seam where the roll ends. With a serrated knife, cut the dough log into slices about 1¾ inches wide. Place flat-side down on the prepared pan, with the sides barely touching. Cover loosely with plastic wrap and let rest for about 30 minutes.

Meanwhile, preheat the oven to 400 degrees F. Uncover the rolls and bake for 10–12 minutes, or until golden brown.

While the rolls bake, beat together the cream cheese, ¼ cup of butter, powdered sugar, coffee, and vanilla with an electric mixer. Spread over the hot cinnamon rolls and serve.

Coffee-Ginger Pancakes

xxxxxx

Hazelnut flour is available in some gourmet markets and health-food stores. If you can't find it, toast about ¼ cup of hazelnuts in a dry skillet until they become aromatic, then remove the skins by placing the nuts in a clean dish towel and rubbing them together. Place the cooled nuts in a food processor and pulse until very finely chopped.

Whisk together the flour, baking powder, cocoa, espresso powder, ginger, cinnamon, and cloves in a large bowl; stir in the hazelnuts.

In a medium bowl, mix the milk, egg whites, molasses, and vegetable oil. Pour this mixture into the dry ingredients. Stir until moistened, but do not over-mix. The batter will be lumpy.

Coat a skillet or griddle with nonstick cooking spray and place over medium-high heat. Using a ¼-cup measure, scoop batter onto the griddle. When bubbles form all over the pancakes, flip and continue to cook until done.

Serves 4

1½ cups all-purpose flour

3 tablespoons baking powder

1½ teaspoons cocoa powder

1½ teaspoons espresso powder

¾ teaspoon ground ginger

½ teaspoon ground cinnamon

½ teaspoon ground cloves

3 tablespoons ground hazelnuts or hazelnut flour

1½ cups milk

3 egg whites

3 tablespoons unsulphured molasses

3 tablespoons vegetable oil

Cooking spray

Coffee for Lunch or Dinner

XXXXXX

Coffee Fajita Marinade

xxxxxx

This makes a great marinade for chicken or skirt steak.

Combine all ingredients in a large plastic zipper bag. Add up to 2 pounds of chicken or skirt steak, cut into strips. Seal the bag and let the meat marinate for at least 1 hour and as long as 24 hours before grilling or sautéing.

Makes enough for 2 pounds of meat

¼ cup apple cider vinegar

2 tablespoons brewed coffee

2 tablespoons Worcestershire sauce

2 tablespoons liquid smoke

2 tablespoons soy sauce

1 tablespoon brown sugar

3 cloves garlic, minced or put through a garlic press

½ teaspoon dried oregano

½ teaspoon freshly ground black pepper

½ teaspoon salt

½ teaspoon lemon pepper seasoning

¼ teaspoon ground cumin

Espresso-Chile Steak Rub

xxxxxx

Makes about ⅓ cup (enough for 2 large steaks)

4 teaspoons espresso powder

1 teaspoon granulated garlic

1½ teaspoons freshly ground black pepper

1 teaspoon salt

1 teaspoon smoked paprika

1 teaspoon dried oregano

½ teaspoon dried thyme

¼ teaspoon ground dried chipotle chile

The dark color of the rub gives a "blackened" effect—a nice contrast to the pink of a steak cooked to a perfect medium or medium-rare.

Mix together all ingredients in a small bowl. Thickly coat steaks with the mixture before grilling or broiling.

Cocoa-Coffee Spice Rub

xxxxxx

The Mayans used chocolate as a savory drink long before the advent of candy, so the use of cocoa as a spice makes perfect sense. This is especially good on pork roast.

Mix together all ingredients in a small bowl. Thickly coat pork roast or steak before grilling or roasting. Extra spice rub can be stored in a sealed plastic bag for six months at room temperature.

Makes about 1 cup

6 tablespoons paprika

2 tablespoons salt

2 tablespoons cocoa powder

2 tablespoons espresso powder

2 tablespoons granulated garlic

2 tablespoons brown sugar

1 tablespoon freshly ground black pepper

Chili with a Coffee Kick

xxxxxx

Serves 6–8

2 tablespoons olive or canola oil

1 large yellow onion, chopped

5 cloves garlic, chopped

3 pounds ground round or other lean ground beef (or ground turkey)

1 can (14½ ounces) diced tomatoes or tomato sauce

1 cup brewed coffee

1 bottle (12 ounces) beer, preferably a dark beer such as bock

1 tablespoon chili powder blend, such as Mexene

1 teaspoon dried oregano

1 teaspoon freshly ground black pepper

1 teaspoon salt

½ teaspoon ground dried chipotle chile

½ teaspoon ground cumin

¼ teaspoon smoked paprika

¼ teaspoon cayenne pepper (optional)

The state dish of Texas—chili—varies from cook to cook. But one thing is always a given: Texas chili is never cooked with beans, although pintos are sometimes served on the side. You could use ground turkey in place of the beef (but again, never in Texas!).

Heat a sauté pan or Dutch oven over medium-high heat. Add oil and onion and cook until soft and translucent, about 5–8 minutes. Add garlic and ground beef and cook until the meat is no longer pink. Lower the heat to medium-low and stir in the tomatoes or tomato sauce, coffee, beer, chili powder, oregano, pepper, salt, chipotle chile, cumin, paprika, and cayenne (if desired). Let the chili simmer for at least an hour to allow flavors to meld. Taste and adjust seasonings as needed.

Coffee Barbecue Sauce

xxxxxx

Makes about 1 cup

½ cup ketchup

¼ cup brewed coffee

2 tablespoons orange juice concentrate

1 tablespoon honey

1½ teaspoons liquid smoke

1 teaspoon soy sauce

1 teaspoon freshly ground black pepper

½ teaspoon salt

¼–½ teaspoon chipotle-flavored Tabasco sauce

This is especially good on the tender pork ribs known as baby-backs, but also try this on grilled steaks or other meats.

Combine all ingredients in a small bowl and mix well. Use as a basting sauce for grilled meats in the last 5 minutes of cooking time to prevent flare-ups and burned meat.

Ham and Red-Eye Gravy

xxxxxx

Serves 8

2 tablespoons unsalted butter

1½ pounds boneless ham steak

1 cup brewed coffee

3 tablespoons brown sugar

This is a classic dish, but with a twist. The coffee provides a contrast to the sweetness of the ham and brown sugar.

Heat the butter in a large skillet or sauté pan. Add the ham and cook until heated through. Remove the ham and place on a serving plate. Add coffee and brown sugar to the pan drippings and heat until the mixture is bubbly and the sugar is dissolved. Pour over the ham steak.

Cowboy Pinto Beans

xxxxxx

Before cooking dried beans, always pour them out onto a baking pan and pick through them to remove any small stones, dirt clods, broken beans, or other detritus.

Drain the beans. Place in a 2-quart saucepan and cover with 2 inches of water. Add the salt pork or bacon, onion, bell pepper, garlic, jalapeño, cumin, tomato sauce or diced tomatoes, and coffee. Bring to a boil. Reduce heat and simmer for at least 2 hours, or until beans are very tender. Add salt to taste, but only after the beans are completely soft.

Serves 4

2 cups pinto beans, soaked overnight in cold water to cover

½ pound salt pork or 4 slices thick-cut bacon, chopped

½ cup chopped onion

½ cup chopped bell pepper (red or green)

2 cloves garlic, chopped or put through garlic press

1 jalapeño, chopped

2 teaspoons ground cumin

1 can (8 ounces) tomato sauce or petite diced tomatoes

1 cup brewed coffee

Salt

Espresso-Marinated Pork Chops

xxxxxx

Serves 4 *Try this marinade on steaks, too.*

4 boneless pork chops

¼ cup brewed
espresso, cooled to
room temperature

¼ cup honey

1 tablespoon soy sauce

1 tablespoon dry sherry

1 clove garlic,
minced or put through
garlic press

½ teaspoon salt

1 teaspoon freshly
ground black pepper

Place the pork chops in a large plastic food-storage bag. In a small bowl, mix together the espresso, honey, soy sauce, sherry, garlic, salt, and pepper. Pour into the bag with the pork chops. Place in the refrigerator and let marinate at least 4 hours and as long as 24 hours. When ready to cook, remove the pork chops from the marinade and grill until done, or an instant-read thermometer indicates that the internal temperature of the pork has reached 160 degrees F.

Coffee for Dessert

XXXXXX

Coffee Biscotti

xxxxxx

Makes 4 dozen

Cooking spray

2¼ cups all-purpose flour

2 teaspoons espresso powder

1 teaspoon baking powder

½ teaspoon baking soda

½ teaspoon ground cinnamon

¼ teaspoon salt

1 cup sugar

2 eggs

2 egg yolks

½ teaspoon vanilla extract

1 cup sliced almonds

These twice-baked Italian cookies will keep for at least a couple of weeks if stored well-wrapped, such as in a plastic zipper bag with excess air squeezed out or in an airtight plastic container or cookie tin.

Preheat the oven to 350 degrees F. Coat a baking sheet with nonstick cooking spray or line with parchment paper.

In a large bowl, whisk together the flour, espresso powder, baking powder, baking soda, cinnamon, and salt.

Whisk the sugar, eggs, and egg yolks until smooth and light colored. Stir in vanilla. Add the dry ingredients and the almonds to the bowl and fold together gently.

Divide the dough in half and form each half into a wide log, about 12 inches long by 2 inches wide. Place in the oven and bake for about 35–40 minutes, or until the logs begin to brown and small cracks appear on the tops. Remove from the oven and let cool for about 10 minutes.

With a serrated knife, cut each loaf into ½-inch slices. Lay the slices cut-side-up onto the baking pan and return to the oven for about 8 minutes. Remove from the oven and flip each cookie over. Return to oven and bake for about 7–8 minutes more. Cookies should be lightly toasted and starting to dry out. Remove from the pan and let cool completely on a wire rack.

Café au Lait Cookies

xxxxxx

The white chocolate chips and coffee in this thin, crisp cookie remind me of a classic coffee-and-cream combination.

Preheat the oven to 350 degrees F. Coat two baking sheets with nonstick cooking spray or line with parchment paper.

Cream together the butter, sugar, and coffee crystals. Add the egg and vanilla, mixing thoroughly after each addition. Stir in the flour until no white streaks remain. Fold in the white chocolate chips.

Drop the cookie mixture by tablespoonfuls onto the prepared pan, spacing the cookies about 3 inches apart. Bake for 10–12 minutes, or until the cookies begin to brown around the edges. Remove from the oven and let cool for about 2 minutes. Transfer to wire racks and let cool completely.

Makes 1½ dozen cookies

Cooking spray

½ cup unsalted butter

⅔ cup granulated sugar

2 tablespoons instant coffee crystals

1 egg

1 teaspoon vanilla extract

¾ cup all-purpose flour

½ cup white chocolate chips

Mocha Thins

xxxxxx

For the crispy-cookie lover. Try sandwiching two of these cookies with Nutella, a hazelnut-chocolate spread, or marshmallow cream. Note that you will need to have parchment paper or silicone baking mats on hand for this recipe.

Makes 4 dozen cookies

2 teaspoons instant coffee powder

1 teaspoon water

1 cup unsalted butter

1 cup sugar

6 tablespoons cocoa powder

¼ teaspoon ground cinnamon

1 egg

1 teaspoon vanilla extract

2 cups all-purpose flour, plus additional for work surface

In a small bowl, mix together the coffee powder and water. Set aside.

Beat the butter and sugar together with an electric mixer until the mixture is light in color and fluffy. Add the cocoa powder, cinnamon, egg, vanilla, and prepared coffee powder–water mixture. Beat until well combined. Stir in the flour until just mixed.

Divide the dough in half, roll each portion into a ball, and flatten into disk shapes. Wrap in plastic wrap and chill until firm, at least 1 hour.

Preheat the oven to 375 degrees F. Line the baking pans with parchment paper or silicone baking mats. Do not grease.

Sprinkle a work surface with a light coating of flour. Roll out one disk of dough to about ⅛ inch thick and cut out with cookie cutters. Place cookies at least one inch apart on the prepared baking sheets. Bake for about 8 minutes or until crisp. Be careful not to let cookies burn, which is easy to do because the dough is dark to begin with. Remove from the oven and cool completely on wire racks. Store in an airtight container.

Mocha Meringues

xxxxxx

Makes about 4 dozen cookies

½ cup sugar

¼ cup cocoa powder

2 teaspoons instant coffee crystals

4 egg whites, at room temperature

½ teaspoon cream of tartar

1 teaspoon vanilla extract

These crisp treats are sometimes called "forgotten cookies," because you leave them in the oven to cool.

Preheat the oven to 250 degrees F. Line 2 baking sheets with foil or parchment paper.

Sift together the sugar, cocoa powder, and instant coffee crystals. Set aside.

Beat the egg whites at medium speed until foamy. Add cream of tartar and vanilla and turn the mixer to high speed until soft peaks form when the beater is lifted. Gradually add the sugar mixture to the egg whites, and continue beating until stiff peaks form.

With a flexible spatula, scoop the meringue mixture into a gallon-size plastic storage bag. Cut across one corner to create a piping bag. Squeeze out small mounds of meringue onto prepared baking sheets. The cookies will not spread or rise, so they can be piped fairly close together, though they should not touch.

Bake for 40 minutes, or until the meringues are firm. Turn off the heat, but leave the pans in the oven until cool (at least 1 hour).

No-Bake Coffee-Oatmeal Bites

xxxxxx

Makes 2 dozen cookies

½ cup unsalted
butter, softened

⅔ cup sugar

3 tablespoons cocoa
powder, preferably
Dutch-process

1 tablespoon strong
brewed coffee, plus
additional if needed
to moisten dough

½ teaspoon vanilla extract

¾ cup quick-cooking oats
(not instant)

½ cup powdered sugar

This one-bowl cookie dough keeps well for several days, stored in an airtight container in the refrigerator.

In a mixing bowl, cream together the butter and sugar until it is light-colored and fluffy. Stir in the cocoa powder, coffee, vanilla, and oats until well mixed. Place the powdered sugar in a small bowl. Roll rounded tablespoons of dough into balls, then coat them with powdered sugar. Place each cookie in a small paper baking cup. Place in an airtight container and store in the refrigerator. Bring to room temperature to serve.

Coffee-Toffee Cookies

xxxxxx

If you can't find toffee bits in the baking aisle of the super-market, try chopping up a few chocolate-covered toffee candy bars, like Heath, to add to the dough.

Preheat the oven to 325 degrees F. Line the baking pans with parchment paper or coat with nonstick cooking spray. In a small bowl, mix the espresso powder in with the coffee liqueur and set aside.

In a large bowl, cream together the butter, sugar, and brown sugar until light colored and fluffy. Add eggs one at a time, mixing well after each addition. Add the reserved espresso mixture and mix well. Sift the flour, cocoa, baking soda, and salt onto a piece of parchment or wax paper. Stir these dry ingredients into the butter mixture. Stir in the toffee bits and chocolate chunks.

Using a tablespoon, drop mounds of dough about two inches apart onto the prepared baking pans. Bake for about 25 minutes, checking often after about 20 minutes, because the cookies are so dark it is easy to burn them. Remove them from the baking pans and let cool completely on wire racks.

Makes 3 dozen cookies

Cooking spray

2 teaspoons instant espresso powder

2 tablespoons coffee liqueur

1 cup unsalted butter, softened

1 cup sugar

¾ cup brown sugar

2 eggs

2½ cups all-purpose flour

⅓ cup cocoa powder

½ teaspoon baking soda

¼ teaspoon salt

1 cup toffee bits

2 cups semisweet chocolate chunks

Coffee Liqueur Brownies

xxxxxx

Serves 9

Cooking spray

1 cup semisweet
chocolate chips

¼ cup unsalted butter

⅔ cup all-purpose flour

½ cup sugar

⅛ teaspoon baking soda

1 tablespoon instant coffee

1 egg

1 egg yolk

1 tablespoon coffee liqueur

1 teaspoon vanilla extract

*These rich, chewy brownies don't need frosting, but you could
sprinkle a little powdered sugar on top to serve.*

Preheat the oven to 350 degrees F. Coat an 8-inch-square pan
with nonstick cooking spray.

In a microwave-safe dish, heat the chocolate chips and butter
at medium power in the microwave for 30 seconds. Remove
and stir. Repeat in 15-second increments until the chocolate is
melted and smooth. Set aside.

In a bowl, whisk together the flour, sugar, and baking soda.
Add the reserved chocolate mixture, instant coffee, egg, egg
yolk, coffee liqueur, and vanilla, and stir just until combined.
Bake for 20–25 minutes. Remove from the oven and set the
pan on a wire rack to cool completely.

Coffee-Molasses Bars

xxxxxx

Makes 24 servings

Cooking spray

½ cup unsalted butter

½ cup granulated sugar

1 egg

½ cup molasses

⅓ cup hot, brewed
coffee or espresso

1½ cups all-purpose flour

1½ teaspoons baking powder

¼ teaspoon baking soda

2 teaspoons
ground cinnamon

½ cup raisins

1 Coffee Glaze recipe
(recipe follows)

These spicy bar cookies topped with coffee-flavored icing make a delicious afternoon treat with a hot cup of coffee or cut into elegant triangles for a special dessert. The Coffee Glaze recipe that follows is perfect with the Coffee-Molasses Bars or as a topping for a Bundt cake.

Preheat the oven to 350 degrees F. Coat a 9 x 13-inch baking pan with nonstick cooking spray.

Cream together the butter and sugar until light and fluffy. Add the egg, molasses, and coffee, and mix, scraping down the sides of the bowl often.

In another mixing bowl, whisk together the flour, baking powder, baking soda, and cinnamon. Add to the butter mixture and beat until thoroughly blended. Stir in the raisins. Pour into the prepared baking pan, smoothing the mixture with a spatula.

Bake for about 25 minutes, or until the bars are firm. Remove from the oven and place the pan on a wire rack. Glaze bars while still warm with Coffee Glaze.

COFFEE GLAZE

¼ cup unsalted butter

2 cups powdered sugar

2 tablespoons cold brewed
coffee or espresso

1 teaspoon vanilla extract

Beat the butter, sugar, coffee, and vanilla together until smooth. Spread the glaze over Coffee-Molasses Bars with a small spatula. Allow the bars to cool completely before cutting into serving-size pieces.

Date-Nut Coffee Loaf

xxxxxx

Leftovers of this loaf are delicious when sliced, toasted, and buttered. You can substitute almost any nut for the pecans in this recipe.

Preheat the oven to 350 degrees F. Coat an 8 x 4-inch loaf pan with butter. Line the bottom only of the pan with a piece of parchment paper cut to fit, and coat it with butter.

Place the dates in a small bowl and sprinkle with the baking soda. Heat the coffee to boiling and pour over the dates and soda. Set aside to soften.

In a mixing bowl, beat together the butter, sugar, and egg until well blended. Scrape down the sides of the bowl. Stir in the vanilla, then the flour and salt. The mixture will look pebbly. Fold in the date-coffee mixture until just combined. Stir in the pecans.

Scrape the mixture into the prepared pan. Bake for 1 hour or until a wooden skewer inserted into the center of the loaf comes out clean. The top of the loaf will spring back when lightly touched. Remove from oven and let cool for 5 minutes. Remove the loaf from the pan, then allow to cool completely on a wire rack.

Makes 1 loaf

2 tablespoons unsalted butter, softened, plus additional for coating pan

1 cup chopped pitted dates

1 teaspoon baking soda

1 cup espresso or strong brewed coffee

1 cup sugar

1 egg

2 teaspoons vanilla extract

1½ cups all-purpose flour

1 teaspoon salt

1 cup chopped pecans

Mocha Cake

xxxxxx

Serves 12

1 tablespoon unsalted
butter, for pan

2 teaspoons cocoa
powder, for pan

2 cups all-purpose flour

2 cups sugar

¾ cup cocoa powder,
preferably natural

1 teaspoon baking powder

2 teaspoons baking soda

⅛ teaspoon salt

½ cup canola oil

1 cup whole milk

1 teaspoon vanilla extract

1 cup hot, brewed coffee

2 eggs, lightly beaten
with a fork

Here is the ideal layer cake for birthdays and other celebra-tions. Try it with the Cappuccino-Cream Cheese Frosting (recipe follows).

Preheat the oven to 325 degrees F. Coat two 9-inch round pans with the butter and dust with 2 teaspoons cocoa powder. Tap out excess cocoa powder and discard.

In a mixing bowl, whisk together the flour, sugar, ¾ cup of cocoa, baking powder, baking soda, and salt. In another bowl, mix the oil, milk, vanilla, coffee, and eggs. Combine the liquid ingredients with the dry ingredients and mix well. (Batter will be thin.)

Pour batter into the prepared pans. Bake for 30–35 minutes, or until a wooden skewer inserted in the middle of the cakes comes out clean. The tops will spring back when lightly touched with a finger. Remove from oven and let cool about 5 minutes. Remove from the pans and let the layers cool completely on wire racks. Frost with Cappuccino–Cream Cheese Frosting.

*Makes enough
for 1 cake*

8 ounces cream cheese

½ cup unsalted
butter, softened

1 teaspoon vanilla extract

3 cups powdered sugar, sifted

2 tablespoons instant
cappuccino mix

CAPPUCCINO–CREAM CHEESE FROSTING

Created for the Mocha Cake, this frosting also would taste great on a pan of brownies or a sheet cake.

Beat together the cream cheese, butter, vanilla, powdered sugar, and instant cappuccino mix until smooth and creamy. Frost the cooled cake layers.

Honey 'n' Coffee Cake

xxxxxx

Serves 24

Cooking spray
4 eggs, separated
¾ cup sugar
⅓ cup canola oil
1 cup honey
3 cups all-purpose flour
½ teaspoon salt
2 teaspoons baking powder
1 teaspoon baking soda
¼ teaspoon ground cloves
½ teaspoon ground allspice
1 cup brewed coffee

This spicy snack cake tastes great with a cup of tea or coffee (of course), but continues to improve with age. Keep it in a tin or wrapped well with foil or plastic, and it will stay delicious for a week.

Preheat the oven to 325 degrees F. Coat two pans (8 x 8-inch) with nonstick cooking spray and lightly dust with flour.

In a mixing bowl, beat the egg yolks with the sugar until creamy and light colored. Add the oil and beat well. Repeat with the honey. The mixture should be smooth. In another bowl, whisk together the flour, salt, baking powder, baking soda, cloves, and allspice. Add about a third of the dry ingredients to the butter mixture, then a third of the coffee, stirring together only until blended. Repeat with the remaining ingredients, alternating dry with coffee. Do not over-mix or the cakes will be dry and tough.

Whip the egg whites until stiff peaks form when the beater is lifted. Fold a third of the egg whites into the batter, repeating until it is all gently incorporated. Some white streaks are fine. Pour the batter into the prepared pans and bake for about 35–40 minutes, or until a wooden skewer inserted into the center of the cakes comes out clean. Remove and let cool completely in the pans on wire racks.

Chocolate Cake with Coffee Frosting

xxxxxx

This moist chocolate sheet cake is topped with a thick layer of rich, coffee frosting.

Preheat the oven to 350 degrees F. Coat a 9 x 13-inch baking pan with nonstick cooking spray.

In a mixing bowl, whisk together the flour, baking soda, and salt. Set aside. Place the oats in a heatproof mixing bowl. Pour boiling water over the oats, then sprinkle with the chocolate chips. Do not stir. Let stand for 20 minutes.

Cream the butter, sugar, and brown sugar at medium-high speed until light and fluffy. Add the eggs, one at a time, then the vanilla, beating well after each addition. Pour in the oat mixture and beat until well combined. Stir in the flour mixture until the batter is smooth and no streaks remain.

Pour the cake batter into the prepared pan. Bake for 35–40 minutes, or until a wooden skewer inserted near the center of the cake comes out clean. Remove from the oven and let the pan cool on a wire rack.

To make the frosting, dissolve the coffee crystals in the warm half-and-half. Cream the butter until light and fluffy. Add the 2 teaspoons of vanilla, salt, and powdered sugar. Beat in the cream mixture, adding only enough to create a soft frosting suitable for spreading on the cake. When cake has cooled completely, ice the top of the cake with the frosting.

Makes 20 servings

Cooking spray

1½ cups all-purpose flour

1 teaspoon baking soda

1 teaspoon salt

1 cup old-fashioned oats

1½ cups boiling water

1 cup semisweet chocolate chips

½ cup unsalted butter, softened

¾ cup sugar

¾ cup light brown sugar

2 eggs

1 teaspoon vanilla extract

2 teaspoons instant coffee crystals

⅓ cup half-and-half, warmed

½ cup unsalted butter, softened

2 teaspoons vanilla extract

1/8 teaspoon salt

4 cups powdered sugar

Cappuccino Cheesecake

xxxxxx

Cheesecakes always develop the best texture and flavor after resting at least overnight in the refrigerator, so make this dessert in advance.

Preheat the oven to 350 degrees F. Coat a 10-inch springform pan with the tablespoon of butter.

Combine the graham cracker crumbs, ¼ cup of butter, 2 tablespoons of sugar, and the cinnamon, and mix well. Gently press the crumb mixture into the bottom of the prepared pan and set aside.

In a small saucepan, gradually heat the semisweet chocolate and heavy whipping cream together until the chocolate is melted, stirring frequently. Stir until smooth. Set aside to cool.

In a mixing bowl, beat the cream cheese until smooth. Slowly add the cup of sugar, mixing until well blended. Add the eggs one at a time. Beat until very smooth. Add the reserved chocolate mixture and blend well. Add the sour cream, salt, coffee, liqueur, and vanilla. Mix until smooth. Do not over-beat or the cheesecake will form cracks in the top. Pour into the prepared pan.

Bake for 45 minutes or until the cheesecake is slightly jiggly in the center when shaken gently. Leave the cake in the oven and prop open the door with the handle of a wooden spoon to allow the cheesecake to cool slowly and help prevent cracks from forming on top of the cake. Remove from the oven and chill for at least 12 hours before serving.

Makes 16 servings

1 tablespoon
unsalted butter

1 cup chocolate graham
cracker crumbs

¼ cup unsalted
butter, softened

2 tablespoons sugar

¼ teaspoon
ground cinnamon

8 ounces
semisweet chocolate

2 tablespoons heavy
whipping cream

24 ounces cream
cheese, softened

1 cup sugar

3 eggs

1 cup sour cream

¼ teaspoon salt

¼ cup brewed coffee, cold

¼ cup coffee liqueur

2 teaspoons vanilla extract

3 C's Sheet Cake

xxxxx

Serves 15–18

Cooking spray

2 cups all-purpose flour

1½ cups brown sugar

1 teaspoon baking soda

1 teaspoon
ground cinnamon

½ teaspoon salt

1 cup unsalted butter

1 cup brewed coffee

¼ cup cocoa powder,
preferably natural

⅓ cup sweetened
condensed milk

2 eggs, lightly beaten
with a fork

1 teaspoon vanilla extract

Coffee, cinnamon, and chocolate give this sheet cake its name. Use the following Espresso Glaze as a sweet topping.

Preheat the oven to 350 degrees F. Coat a 10 x 15-inch jelly-roll pan with nonstick cooking spray and lightly dust with flour.

In a mixing bowl, whisk together the flour, brown sugar, baking soda, cinnamon, and salt. Set aside.

In a small saucepan, melt the butter over medium heat. Add the coffee and cocoa powder and mix well. Add this mixture to the dry ingredients in the mixing bowl. Stir in the condensed milk, eggs, and vanilla. Mix until smooth and blended.

Pour the batter into the prepared pan. Bake for 15–20 minutes, or until the top springs back when lightly touched. Remove from the oven and place on a wire rack.

Prepare the Espresso Glaze (recipe follows) and spread it on while the cake is still warm.

*Makes enough for 1
sheet cake*

ESPRESSO GLAZE

¼ cup unsalted butter

¼ cup cocoa powder

2 teaspoons espresso powder

⅔ cup sweetened
condensed milk

1 cup powdered sugar

Melt the butter in a small saucepan. Add the cocoa powder, espresso powder, and condensed milk. Beat in the powdered sugar.

Mocha Ice Cream

xxxxxx

The custard base of the ice cream is best made the day before the ice cream is churned, in order to allow the flavors to blend and mellow.

Place a strainer over a mixing bowl.

Heat the milk, whipping cream, coffee, and ½ cup of the sugar in a saucepan over medium-high heat, stirring frequently, until the sugar is dissolved but the mixture does not boil. Add the chocolate and stir until melted.

In a small bowl, beat the egg yolks and the remaining ¼ cup of sugar. Slowly add about a cup of the warm milk mixture to the egg yolks and whisk until incorporated. Add the egg yolk mixture back into the saucepan with the rest of the milk mixture, and continue to cook until the custard reaches 180 degrees F on an instant-read thermometer.

Remove the saucepan from the heat and pour the custard through the strainer placed over the bowl. Allow the custard to cool slightly. Place plastic wrap over the bowl, pressing down the plastic until it is in direct contact with the custard. This is to prevent a "skin" from forming on the custard. Refrigerate at least 8 hours or overnight.

Place the custard in an ice-cream maker and churn according to the manufacturer's instructions. Any leftover ice cream should be transferred to a freezer-safe container and frozen.

Makes about 1 quart

1 cup whole milk

2 cups heavy whipping cream

3 tablespoons instant coffee

¾ cup granulated sugar, divided

3½ ounces bittersweet chocolate in bar form, broken into small pieces

4 egg yolks

Mocha Pots de Crème

xxxxxx

Makes 12 servings

2 eggs

1 package (12 ounces) semisweet chocolate chips

⅓ cup sugar

1 teaspoon vanilla extract

2 tablespoons coffee liqueur, or more to taste

Pinch of salt

1 cup whole milk

Whipped cream, for garnish (optional)

This quick and easy dessert, using a technique I first learned from my friend Linda, is fancy enough for a dinner party.

Put the eggs, chocolate chips, sugar, vanilla, coffee liqueur, and salt in a blender.

Bring the milk to a simmer on the stove.

Pour the hot milk into the blender while blending. Blend for 1–2 minutes. Make sure the chocolate is melted and you start to see some bubbles form. (The hot milk cooks the eggs.)

Pour into individual dessert dishes and chill. Top with whipped cream before serving, if desired.

Mocha Fudge

xxxxxx

This recipe uses a couple of shortcuts—sweetened condensed milk, the microwave—but the results are long on flavor. Paper candy cups can be purchased as party supplies or in the cake-decorating departments of hobby and craft stores.

Makes 16 pieces

2 cups semisweet chocolate chips or chopped baking squares

1 can (14 ounces) sweetened condensed milk

1 tablespoon espresso powder

1 teaspoon vanilla extract

Pinch of salt

Line an 8-inch square baking pan with aluminum foil and set aside.

In a microwave-safe bowl, combine the chocolate, condensed milk, and espresso powder. Heat on medium-high to high power in the microwave, stopping every 30 seconds to stir the mixture until the chocolate is melted and smooth. Watch closely, because chocolate burns easily.

Remove from the microwave and stir in the vanilla and salt. Pour into the prepared pan and chill for several hours. When the fudge is firm, remove it from the pan. Peel off the foil and cut the fudge into small squares. Place the pieces in paper candy cups for gift giving. Store the fudge, well wrapped, in the refrigerator until ready to serve.

Gifts for Coffee Lovers

xxxxxx

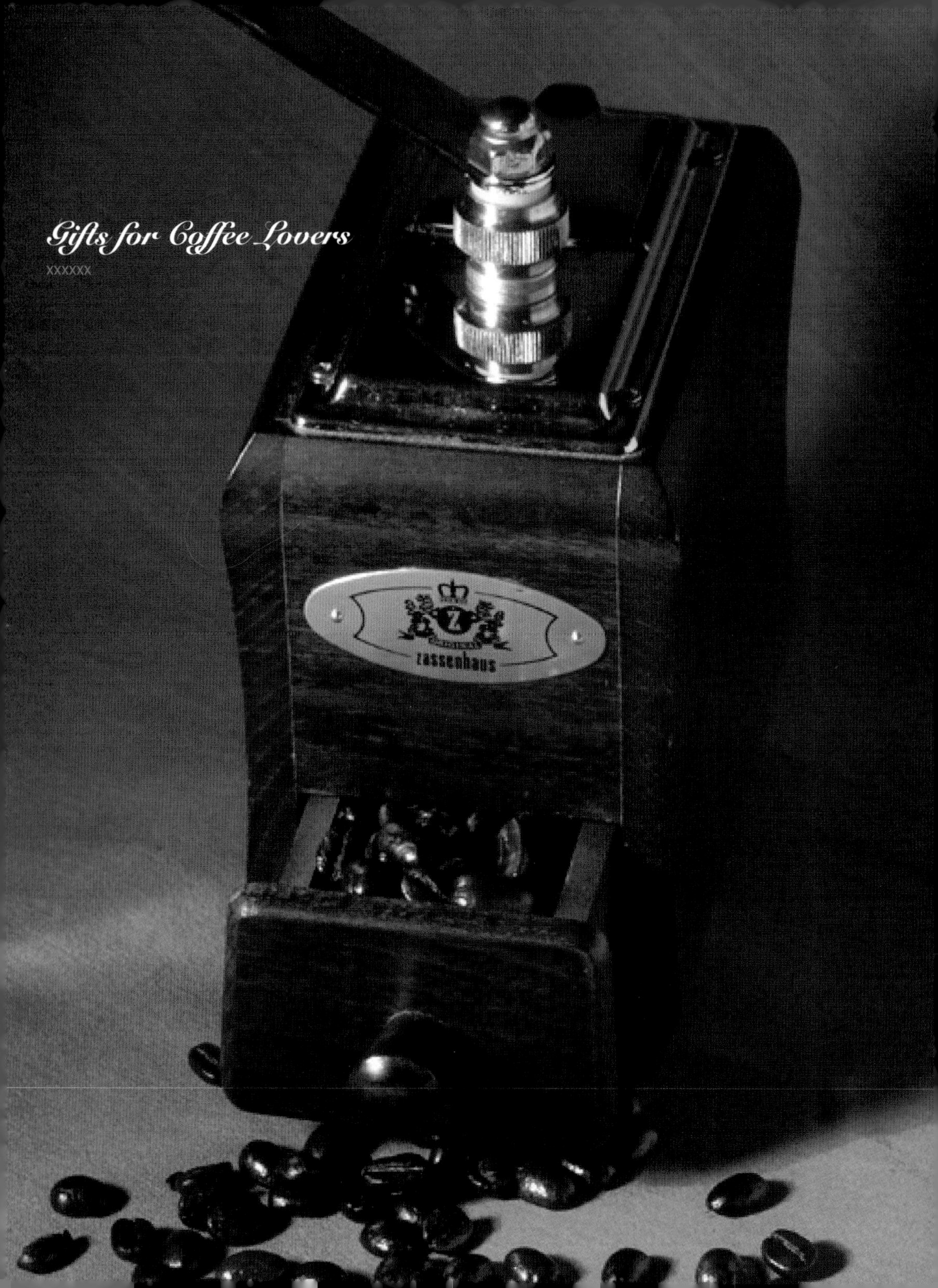

Coffee Liqueur

xxxxxx

It takes a while for the flavors to develop, but it's worth the wait. This liqueur makes an ideal do-ahead holiday gift. Decorative, food-safe bottles can be purchased at gourmet shops or the housewares section of department and specialty stores. You'll need bottles with lids such as screw-on caps or tight-fitting corks to help prevent evaporation.

Makes about 6½ cups

2 ounces espresso powder

3½ cups sugar

2 cups boiling water

1 pint vodka

1 whole vanilla bean

Clean and sterilize two 26-ounce glass bottles. Set aside.

In a large, heatproof bowl, mix the espresso powder and sugar. Stir in the boiling water until the sugar is dissolved. Allow to cool to room temperature. Add the vodka.

Split the vanilla bean in half and add one half to each of the prepared bottles. Divide the coffee liqueur evenly between the 2 bottles. Close the bottles tightly. Keep in a cool, dark place for at least a month before serving.

Chocolate Spoons for Coffee

xxxxxx

Makes 12 spoons

1 semisweet chocolate baking bar

12 plastic spoons

Gourmet and gift shops sell these spoons individually wrapped in cellophane, but they are easy to make at home.

Break the chocolate baking bar into small pieces. Place about one-fourth of the chocolate in a small bowl and set aside.

Place the remaining three-fourths of the chocolate in a microwave-safe bowl and heat on medium power in microwave for 30 seconds. Remove from the microwave and stir. Repeat until the chocolate is almost completely melted. Remove the chocolate from the microwave and stir until the chocolate is smooth. Add the reserved unmelted chocolate and stir again until the mixture is completely melted and smooth.

Holding a plastic spoon by the handle, dip the bowl of the spoon in the chocolate until coated completely. Place the spoon on waxed or parchment paper. Repeat with the remaining spoons until the chocolate is gone. If the chocolate is not set completely, place the spoons in the refrigerator for a few minutes. Wrap individually in cellophane and tie with ribbons.

Vanilla Sugar

xxxxxx

Use any type of sugar you prefer. Turbinado sugar, also called "sugar in the raw," is especially nice in coffee.

Makes 4 gifts

2 cups sugar

1 vanilla bean

Place the sugar in a glass jar with a tight-fitting lid. Split the vanilla bean in half, then bury it in the sugar. Close the jar and allow it to sit for at least a month before using sugar. A stronger vanilla flavor can be obtained by grinding the sugar with the whole vanilla bean in a food processor. Close the jar and allow it to sit for at least a month before using sugar. To give as a gift, divide the sugar evenly among four small glass jars with lids. Label.

Homemade Instant Mocha Mix

xxxxxx

Makes 4 gifts

½ cup cocoa powder

¼ cup espresso powder

1 cup sugar

3 cups nonfat dry milk powder

⅛ teaspoon salt

Do not omit the salt—I promise that your mocha will not taste salty. Salt is a flavor enhancer and is important even in sweets.

Sift together the cocoa powder, espresso powder, sugar, milk powder, and salt, sifting three times. Whisk to make sure ingredients are mixed well.

To give as a gift: Divide evenly and scoop into plastic bags or small glass or plastic containers. Attach a card with instructions on how to make the mocha:

To serve: Combine ¼ cup of the mix with hot water or milk in a mug. Stir until dissolved and well mixed.